MOON
Landings

by Barbara Fierman

PEARSON
Scott
Foresman

What You Already Know

The Earth moves in an elliptical path, or orbit, around the Sun. This revolution takes about 365 days. The Moon moves in an elliptical orbit around the Earth. This revolution takes about twenty-eight days, just about one month. The Earth rotates, or spins, on its axis. One rotation takes about twenty-four hours, just about one day.

Our solar system consists of the Sun and its satellites. These satellites include the nine planets, their moons, and other smaller objects. Gravity holds these objects in their orbits. Space probes have been sent from Earth to explore the planets in our solar system.

People who use telescopes to view the solar system often see comets. They appear as moving, fuzzy objects. A comet is actually a frozen mass of ice, dust, and rock that orbits the Sun. Each year, several comets travel in the solar system and orbit the Sun.

Asteroids also revolve around the Sun and are often referred to as minor planets. An asteroid is a mass of rock that can be up to several hundred kilometers wide. Most asteroids travel in the region between Mars and Jupiter.

The Moon is Earth's nearest neighbor in the solar system. It is located about 238,000 miles from Earth. Each month, we see the Moon in different shapes, or Moon phases. Moon phases are the shapes of the lit side of the Moon that we can see on Earth. Sometimes we see the Moon as a whole circle, while at other times we see a half circle, a crescent, or no Moon at all.

a view of Earth from the Moon

In 1968, an Apollo spacecraft was launched into space. The event marked the beginning of Moon exploration by the United States.

The American people wanted to see the Moon close up and explore it. They also wanted to keep up with the progress being made by the U.S.S.R., the Union of Soviet Socialist Republics. This Union was made up of Russia and fourteen neighboring states.

The Soviets sent up the world's first space probe, *Sputnik*, in 1957. In 1961, a Soviet astronaut named Yuri Gagarin orbited the Earth. The Soviets were even able to land a space probe on the Moon.

On May 25, 1961, President John F. Kennedy gave a famous speech in which he challenged Americans to send a person to the Moon.

John F. Kennedy was elected President of the United States in 1960. One of his goals was to send the first humans to the Moon by 1970. In his speech to Congress on May 25, 1961, he challenged Americans to make his goal a reality.

Luna 2 was the first space probe to land on the Moon.

Kennedy knew that the project would be expensive and difficult. Scientists, engineers, pilots, and doctors at the National Aeronautics and Space Administration (NASA) led the effort.

NASA sent fact-finding missions into space. The purpose of these missions was to gather information for the people going to the Moon, so they would know what to expect. NASA sent astronauts into Earth's orbit and brought them back safely during Project Mercury. In Project Gemini astronauts practiced skills that would be needed for a Moon mission. The project that would send astronauts to the Moon and return them safely to Earth was called Apollo.

The Soviet Yuri Gagarin was the first man in space. On April 12, 1961, he orbited the Earth in the spaceship *Vostok 1*.

Reaching the Moon

The Saturn V rocket was the vehicle used to launch the Apollo missions into space. It was the largest, most powerful rocket ever launched by the United States. The rocket was more than 363 feet high, taller than a thirty-six story building! It was designed as a disposable rocket, so a new one had to be built for each Apollo mission.

The Saturn V was made up of three parts, or stages, stacked on top of each other. When the fuel in one stage was used up, it fell off and the next stage took over. The first two stages each had five rocket engines. The third stage had only one.

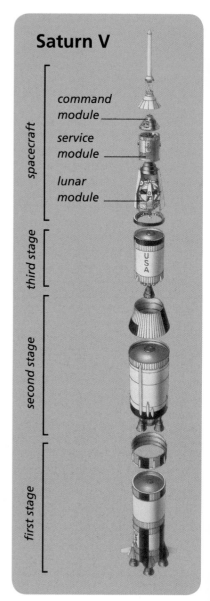

Saturn V

spacecraft
- command module
- service module
- lunar module

third stage

second stage

first stage

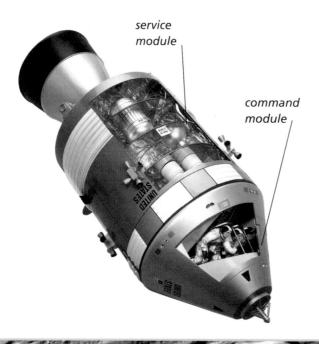

service module

command module

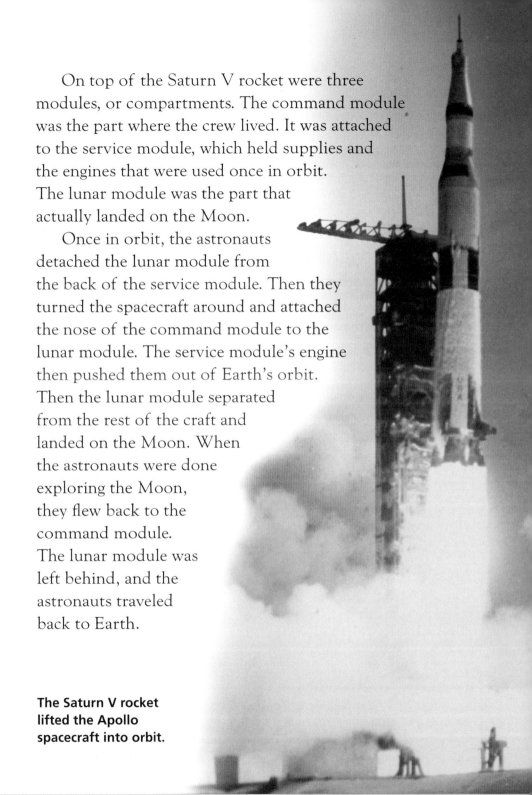

On top of the Saturn V rocket were three modules, or compartments. The command module was the part where the crew lived. It was attached to the service module, which held supplies and the engines that were used once in orbit. The lunar module was the part that actually landed on the Moon.

Once in orbit, the astronauts detached the lunar module from the back of the service module. Then they turned the spacecraft around and attached the nose of the command module to the lunar module. The service module's engine then pushed them out of Earth's orbit. Then the lunar module separated from the rest of the craft and landed on the Moon. When the astronauts were done exploring the Moon, they flew back to the command module. The lunar module was left behind, and the astronauts traveled back to Earth.

The Saturn V rocket lifted the Apollo spacecraft into orbit.

A Giant Leap

Two early missions, *Apollo 7* and *9*, orbited Earth and tested the parts of the Apollo spacecraft. *Apollo 8* and *10* orbited the Moon and photographed the lunar surface. The information gained from these missions set the stage for the historic *Apollo 11* mission.

Neil Armstrong was the first person to step onto the Moon.

On July 16, 1969, a Saturn V rocket launched *Apollo 11* into space. Astronauts Neil Armstrong, Edwin "Buzz" Aldrin, and Michael Collins traveled in the command module *Columbia*. As they neared the Moon, Armstrong and Aldrin crawled into the lunar module *Eagle*. Collins stayed aboard the *Columbia* and orbited the Moon.

The *Apollo 11* crew consisted of mission commander Neil Armstrong, command module pilot Michael Collins, and lunar module pilot Edwin "Buzz" Aldrin.

Neil Armstrong photographed Buzz Aldrin stepping out of the lunar module and onto the Moon.

The lunar module separated from the command module and continued toward the Moon. The excitement back on Earth was high when Armstrong announced, "The *Eagle* has landed."

More than 500 million people watched by television as Armstrong stepped out onto the Moon's surface. They listened as he spoke these now-famous words: "That's one small step for a man; one giant leap for mankind."

Armstrong and Aldrin planted a U.S. flag on the Moon's surface. Since there is no wind on the Moon, they had to use a special flagpole to display the flag.

The astronauts spent about two and a half hours exploring the Moon's surface. They collected forty-four pounds of rock and soil samples to bring back to Earth. According to their descriptions, rocks of all sizes, shapes, and textures are scattered on the Moon. The surface is covered with a fine, gray dust. The dust is packed tightly, however, so the men could walk on it and not sink in.

This photograph shows Buzz Aldrin observing a solar wind experiment.

When the astronauts finished their work, they left their boots, backpacks, and empty food containers on the Moon. The *Eagle*'s rocket blasted them off the Moon. When they reached the *Columbia*, they climbed in to travel back to Earth with Collins. The *Eagle* was allowed to float off into space.

As they approached the Earth, the astronauts released the service module into space and continued to Earth in the command module. Just five months before the deadline, President Kennedy's goal had been achieved. Americans had walked on the Moon and returned safely to Earth.

Back to Earth

On the trip back to Earth, the service module separated from the command module *Columbia*. The *Columbia* splashed down into the Pacific Ocean on July 24, 1969.

Moon Survival

Apollo astronauts needed spacesuits that were suitable for flying in space and walking on the Moon. Since the Moon has no atmosphere, the spacesuit needed to protect the men from heat, cold, and very low pressure. It also had to supply them with oxygen, since there is no air on the Moon. The Apollo spacesuit was made of many layers of special fabrics. The spacesuit and its backpack weighed 180 pounds on Earth, but only 30 pounds on the Moon, because gravity is not very powerful there.

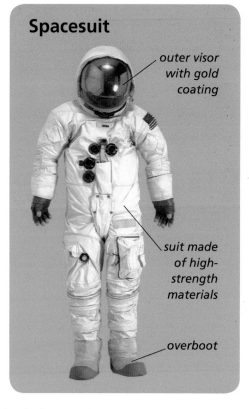

Spacesuit

outer visor with gold coating

suit made of high-strength materials

overboot

An inside layer was made of a lightweight form of nylon. It had water-filled tubes running through it that could be kept hot or cold. This protected the astronauts from the Moon's extreme temperatures. The middle layer was coated with a special material to hold pressure.

Special overboots were designed for walking on the Moon.

The outside layer was made of a tough material to help the suit keep its shape. Since the suit was pressurized, it needed this outer layer to keep it from blowing up like a balloon. It also kept the suit from being torn, which would have been extremely dangerous for the astronauts.

In addition to the spacesuits, astronauts wore boots, gloves, and a helmet. When they walked on the Moon, they added overboots and gloves with rubber fingertips. They also wore visors over their helmets to protect their faces and eyes from the Sun.

Astronauts wore backpacks containing oxygen, cooling water, and special equipment to remove carbon dioxide.

Later Landings

After the historic *Apollo 11* mission, six more Apollo missions were sent to explore the Moon. Five of these missions, *Apollo 12, 14, 15, 16,* and *17,* landed on the Moon. Astronauts collected rock and soil samples, took photographs, and set up experiments to learn more about the Moon.

Apollo 12 was actually hit by lightning just after it was launched, but the astronauts and their equipment were fine. Astronauts Charles Conrad and Alan Bean discovered the *Surveyor III*, a probe that had been sent to the Moon two years earlier. They used instruments called seismographs to measure the movements of the Moon's surface. These instruments also provided information about moonquakes and the effects of meteorites crashing onto the Moon.

On *Apollo 14*, astronauts sketched landmarks on the Moon's surface. They used these sketches to create maps of the Moon. *Apollo 15* astronauts traveled on the Moon's surface in the lunar roving vehicle, a small collapsible car, for the first time. Astronauts on *Apollo 16* conducted experiments to study solar wind on the Moon. In 1972, *Apollo 17* made the last manned lunar landing.

Apollo 12 astronaut Alan Bean shows samples from the Moon.

Apollo 17 astronaut Harrison Schmitt uses special long-handled tools to collect samples from the Moon's surface.

Near Disaster

Apollo 13 was launched on April 11, 1970. Astronauts James Lovell, Fred Haise, and John Swigert were ready for the challenge of Moon exploration. On April 13, however, their mission nearly turned into a disaster. One of their oxygen tanks exploded. The explosion blew out one side of the service module and caused damage to the other oxygen tank.

The astronauts were in great danger. The spacecraft gradually lost oxygen, electricity, light, and water. The astronauts were 200,000 miles away from Earth and had to make quick decisions in order to stay alive.

NASA scientists on Earth kept in contact with the *Apollo 13* astronauts.

NASA scientists on the ground worked quickly to find a solution. They told the *Apollo 13* crew to move into the lunar module and use it as a kind of lifeboat. The lunar module had not been damaged during the explosion, and it contained enough water, oxygen, and power for four days. The module's engine had enough power to send the crew back toward the Earth. When they

After an oxygen tank exploded, the side of the service module blew out, which resulted in a loss of fuel.

got close, they went back into the command module, which was still attached to the lunar module. Only the command module could keep the astronauts safe as they fell through the atmosphere and landed in the ocean.

The three astronauts lost a total of thirty-one pounds, and were tired, hungry, and dehydrated when they returned. But they were alive and would be fine.

The *Apollo 13* crew returned to Earth in the command module, which landed safely on April 17, 1970.

Moon Buggy

On each of the last three Apollo missions, astronauts brought a lunar roving vehicle (LRV) to the Moon. They used the vehicle, also known as a Moon Buggy, to travel around the Moon's surface. The Moon Buggy was designed to travel in the Moon's environment.

In a Moon Buggy, the astronauts could travel as far as six miles away from the lunar module. The vehicle could reach speeds of eleven miles per hour.

The LRV's frame had a hinge in the middle so it could be folded and stored in the lunar module.

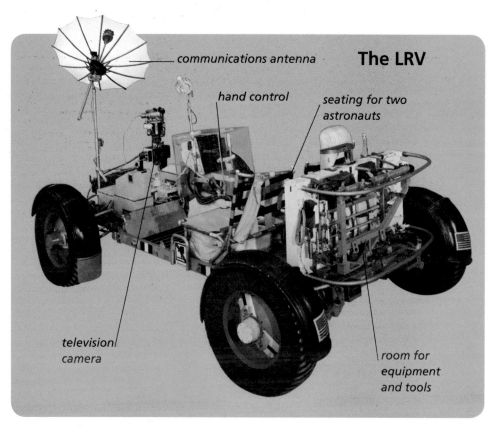

The LRV

communications antenna

hand control

seating for two astronauts

television camera

room for equipment and tools

Each Moon Buggy was battery operated and looked like a golf cart. It was folded up and carried to the Moon in the lunar module, and left on the Moon when the astronauts returned to Earth.

Each Moon Buggy had two folding seats made of aluminum and nylon webbing. An armrest was located between the seats. Each seat had an adjustable footrest and a seatbelt. The buggy was equipped with cameras and tools to record information and gather samples.

Astronauts on the *Apollo 15, 16,* and *17* missions drove the vehicle every day for each of the three days they explored the Moon. In their reports they stated that the LRV was both reliable and safe. It allowed the astronauts to travel longer distances and gather more information than they could have done without it.

Moon Discoveries

The Apollo missions provided valuable scientific information and cleared up some of the mysteries surrounding the Moon. For example, many people believed that the surface of the Moon was like quicksand. The missions showed that the fine soil on the surface is actually well packed.

Astronauts gathered about 840 pounds of rock and soil samples on the six trips they made to the Moon. Geologists analyzed the samples and learned that the Moon is about 4.6 billion years old, about the same age as Earth. Soil samples from the *Apollo 11* mission proved that plants could grow in Moon soil as well as in Earth's soil.

Moon rock

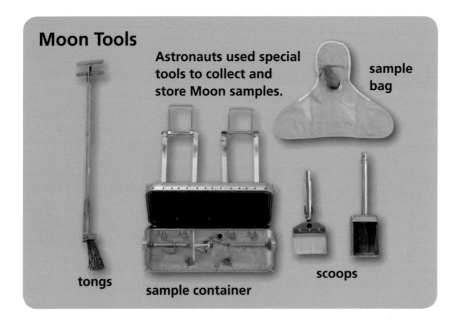

Moon Tools

Astronauts used special tools to collect and store Moon samples.

sample bag

tongs

sample container

scoops

Scientists discovered that about three billion years ago, active volcanoes existed on the Moon. Hot lava spewed from the volcanoes and melted over the Moon's surface. Astronauts from *Apollo 15* and *17* returned with samples of glass beads that were created by volcanic eruptions. Today the volcanoes are no longer active.

Scientists created new technologies for the Apollo missions. Some of these technologies were later used in the invention of personal computers, pocket calculators, and cellular phones. Satellites that were developed for the space program have helped predict weather and crop conditions. Freeze-dried food that was developed for the astronauts is now being used to feed disabled and elderly people.

Scientists examine samples collected on the *Apollo 17* mission. Astronauts spent seventy-five hours on the Moon, exploring and collecting samples.

The Future

Do you think that people will return to the Moon to live in the near future? Scientists are working to try to make this possible. In 1998, the Lunar Prospector orbited the Moon to search for ice on the Moon's poles. Some experiments have suggested that there may be billions of tons of ice on the Moon. The discovery of ice would mean that settlers on the Moon would have the water and oxygen necessary for human life.

The first colony on the Moon might be a mining operation. Satellites have identified important minerals on the Moon that could be mined. The Moon could also be used as a base for further exploration of the solar system.

This artist's view of a lunar colony shows special equipment to protect people from the lack of air on the Moon.

President Kennedy's dream of exploring the Moon became a reality through the Apollo space program. Six missions touched down on the Moon. Twelve astronauts collected Moon samples. Scientists on Earth have analyzed the samples. Perhaps the results of these missions will lead to the development of Moon colonies in the future.

Apollo Missions

Apollo 7	1968 A manned Apollo mission; orbited the Earth 163 times
Apollo 8	1968 A manned spaceship that orbited the Moon
Apollo 9	1969 A manned test of the lunar module; orbited the Earth 151 times
Apollo 10	1969 Mission orbited the Moon; dropped the lunar module within nine miles of the Moon
Apollo 11	1969 First mission to land on the Moon; astronauts took rock samples, planted flag
Apollo 12	1969 Mission was struck by lightning during launch; landed on the Moon and returned safely to Earth
Apollo 13	1970 Oxygen tank exploded; astronauts took shelter in the lunar module; returned safely to Earth in the command module
Apollo 14	1971 Astronauts conducted extensive experiments on the Moon
Apollo 15	1971 Astronauts used lunar roving vehicle for the first time
Apollo 16	1972 A three-day mission; astronauts again drove the LRV
Apollo 17	1972 Last Apollo mission; astronauts stayed on the Moon for about seventy-five hours

Glossary

astronaut   person trained to go into space

colony   population of living things or people

lunar   having to do with the Moon

meteorite   a space rock that crashes into a planet or moon

module   a section of a spacecraft

seismograph   an instrument that measures the movements of the ground

spacecraft   vehicle that travels beyond Earth and into space

solar wind   electrically charged particles released by the Sun

volcano   an opening in a planet's surface through which hot liquid rock is thrown up during an eruption